30 Jewels

Master the Game of Life

30 Jewels

Master the Game of Life

Justin Settles

&

Kenneth Woods

30 Jewels is a registered trademark of w&s, LLC.

Cover photographs (back) taken by Leslie Settles and Brian Carter

Design by Brian Carter

Edited by Rachel Cannon and Claire Dodson

ISBN 978-0-9909027-1-3 (paper), 978-0-9909027-3-7 (ebk)

Proudly Printed in the United States of America

Justin's Acknowledgements

Writing this book is a dream come true. So many people shared in making this possible that I cannot name each individual, but you know who you are. Thanks!

To Amy Baby, you have the same glow as the first day I saw you. Thank you for sharing your kind, warm essence. Let's continue to soar higher and higher.

I am truly blessed to belong to a family that supports, encourages, and uplifts me. Ma, Dad, Leslie, and Champ I love you. Jazz and Jade I see you. Josiah you are next up. Big Ma you continue to be a major inspiration. Gram, I know you are looking down from Heaven smiling!

A special note of love to my Beulah family. You hold a special place in my heart.

Kenneth's Acknowledgements

First, I'd like to thank God for allowing me to complete this book.

Thanks to everyone who helped during the creative process. It took a lot of time, effort, and care to put this piece together.

Above all I would like to thank my family for being a support system for me and giving me the confidence to reach for my dreams: my brothers Kevin and Dietrich, Mom, Dad.

Timothy M. and Josh, thanks for the pointers. Your contribution is very much appreciated.

Contents

Acknowledgements

Introduction

Part 1: Justin Settles

See the Bigger Picture   1

"Welcome to Dixie Queen. May I take your order?"   3

Look Beyond Setbacks   5

What is Your Motivation in Life?   9

How Well are You Managing Your Brand?   11

Build Your Circle of Success   15

Tame Your Doubts and Fears   21

8 Crawl Before You Walk   25

9 Go Hard Every Day   29

10 Celebrate Other People's Blessings   31

11 Help Others Reach New Heights   33

12 Find a Healthy Outlet   35

13 Never Mind the Haters   37

14 You Only Fail When You Stop Trying   39

15 Dare to Dream   41

Part 2: Kenneth Woods

16 Make It Happen 43

17 Read Life's Road Signs 45

18 Follow Your Passion 47

19 Stay Down 'til You Come Up 49

20 Expect More 53

21 Maximize Your Moment 55

22 Complacency is Your Worst Enemy 57

23 Expand Your Hustle 59

24 Losses are Part of the Game 61

25 Be Investable   63

26 Explore the World   65

27 Make Your Money Work for You   67

28 Even if it is Free it will Cost You   75

29 Be a Game Changer   81

30 Run the Score Up   83

The Core Themes of *30 Jewels*   89

Appendixes   95

About the Authors   97

Introduction

30 Jewels was written to help you achieve the purpose-driven life you desire. The book is divided into two parts. Justin Settles delivers Part 1 and Part 2 comes from Kenneth Woods. The book features thirty elements (jewels) we believe will enrich your life. Each jewel is pulled from our personal experiences, situations we encountered, and the lessons we learned. We explain how the jewels have helped us enjoy success in various walks of life at relatively young ages while avoiding a lot of snags along the way.

Now that we have shared our motivation for penning this book, let us briefly explain what we mean by *Master the Game of Life*. As we see it, mastering life involves structuring your time and other resources to be able to pursue the things you are passionate about.

Success is mentioned numerous times throughout the book (forty times to be exact). It is important that you understand success is what you make it. How so? Suppose for a moment that you asked three people how they define success. There's a good chance that success means something different to each person.

For the first person success may involve earning a million dollars. The second individual may say success revolves around family. The third respondent may place a high value on education and take pride in having earned a PhD. Without doubt, these are all great accomplishments. The fact remains that there is no standard definition for what it means to be successful. That's OK because everyone is unique. Your idea of what it means to be successful should reflect what you value most. We leave it to you to determine what success means to you personally.

30 Jewels is based on seven core themes– belief, perseverance, patience, goodwill, time management, positive energy, and empowerment. These seven themes resonate in our lives. If you recognize the power they hold and would like to enhance your reading experience then refer to the Core Themes section at the end of the book.

Believe • Grow • Prosper

Part 1

Justin Settles

See the Bigger Picture

Much truth lies in the saying 'Perception is reality.' This is certainly the case when applied on an individual basis. Your perception shapes the reality in which you live. How is this true? The answer can be found by digging deeper into the saying itself.

Your reality begins with the way you see yourself. Imagine that your self-perception is based on a single photo. So you snap a pic and begin checking it out. You find that it is a nice photo. As you look closer though, you notice a blemish on your shirt. Despite how nice the picture is, focusing on the blemish impacts how you feel about the picture (i.e., your perception of yourself). In this way, perception can be thought of as the portion of the picture you choose to focus on.

Now, consider the following alternative: instead of focusing on the blemish, take in the entire picture. When you do this, you are pleased with your smile and outfit just like before. The blemish is still there. However, you don't let it take center stage this time and you appreciate the picture for everything it has to offer.

When you take in the bigger picture your perception is more positive. You take in the good and the not so good aspects and end up with an outlook that more accurately reflects everything going on in the picture.

TAKEAWAY Be careful not to overlook the positive things going on in your life. Your perception influences your demeanor and the way you engage with others. Be solution-oriented instead of problem-plagued. Looking at the bigger picture may expose angles that change your perception and your reality for the better.

2

"Welcome to Dixie Queen. May I take your order?"

My first 9-to-5 job was working at my mother's Dixie Queen fast food restaurant. Even though my mother owned and operated the shop, I got the full fast food experience– long shifts, standing over the hot fryer, dealing with upset customers, and thinking of every other place I'd rather be sometimes! One night, we were even robbed at gunpoint. That just comes with the territory in the fast food industry, though.

Delivering the best food possible was the top priority. That meant the food had to be fresh and prepared properly. Also, with my mother as my boss and my older sister filling in when she was not there, being late simply was not accepted, so it was important that I showed up on time for shifts. I made sure my uniform was clean each day. I also worked hard to keep the floors, food prep area, and utensils clean. These tasks helped me learn the importance of doing a job the right way and not cutting corners. Even though I traded the fast food kitchen for a career as an economist and educator these lessons still hold true. My goal as an economist is to deliver data users the highest quality products possible to measure economic activity. In the classroom, my goal is to help students from various academic backgrounds understand economic principles and how they are used in the real world.

Working at Dixie Queen was a great stepping stone. The work was hard, but I enjoyed the regular checks. Realistically, there wasn't much else I was qualified to do at seventeen. While the weekly paychecks kept money in my pocket, I never stopped setting goals and striving to achieve more. I realized that earning a college degree would play a pivotal role in helping me achieve more for myself and be able to help others.

TAKEAWAY   You have to be willing to start somewhere. That starting point may not be glamorous. Remember, some opportunities are in your life for a specific season. Make the most of them while they are available to you and apply what you learn going forward.

Look Beyond Setbacks

Life does not always go as planned. Even when you put forth your best effort you may not get the results you anticipated. When this happens you have to be willing to regroup and try again.

Basketball has always been my favorite sport so naturally I had big hoop dreams. I really began taking the game seriously when I was six. I played whenever I could and as time passed my skills improved. Little did I know that a couple years later an injury would threaten my future on the court.

When I was eight years old I suffered a terrible dog bite while playing basketball at a neighbor's house. It was dark out. I reached for a loose ball that rolled under his trampoline unaware that his one hundred-thirty pound Rottweiler was tied to it. Without warning, the dog tore into my arm. Its grip was tight as it wrung my arm from side to side. Blood gushed from my arm and spattered to the ground. My neighbor was frozen with shock and unable to call off his dog. I had to hit the crazed animal in the head to get it to release my arm, but by then the damage had been done. I hopped on my bike and rode home. A trail of my blood stained the sidewalk. It wasn't until I made it to the emergency room that my adrenaline settled and I actually realized how badly I was injured. Layers of flesh had been peeled back to the point that bone was exposed.

The healing process took more than six months and required dozens of doctor visits and procedures. The gaping wound required 150 stitches and doctors told me that I might not ever regain full strength in my right arm.

Despite their predictions, I stayed prayerful. I did as much as I could to help the recovery process and slowly regained strength.

I made the freshman squad my 9th grade year and played on the junior varsity team my sophomore and junior years. After that I transferred schools my senior year and earned a spot on the varsity basketball team. My time on the court would be cut short yet again. After just two games I received a letter notifying me that I was ineligible to play the remainder of the season because I violated the athletic board's transfer policy. This was nothing I had planned for and it forced me to reevaluate things. I stepped back and looked at my situation. I asked myself if all the training, practices, and sacrifices I made were for nothing. Of course not! All that work made me a stronger person and taught me valuable lessons I still carry with me today.

Off the court, my grades were good. I was offered academic scholarships from several colleges. Even though I would not be playing college ball I decided to make the most of the opportunity in front of me and enrolled at The University of Tennessee at Knoxville.

TAKEAWAY Breakthroughs come when you are persistent and relentless in achieving your goal. Stay focused. Understand that your shortcomings do not define you.

Look Beyond Setbacks

4
What is Your Motivation in Life?

Are you talking about it or are you really being about it? Do you *say* you want to be rich but constantly live outside your means? Do you claim to want to be the best at what you do but hit the club every week? It takes hard work and dedication to break through to the upper echelon of your potential. Making some sacrifices today so you see the bigger payoff down the road is part of that. When you set goals you also have to make sure the choices you make are not keeping you from achieving those goals.

To this day, no advice has driven this point home better than words from my grandmother. As she put it, "A goal without a plan is a wish." Sure enough, as I grew older I noticed that some people were always excited to talk about moves they were about to make. At the same time, though, they never actually put any action behind those words. They were just wishing; wishing the things they wanted would fall in their laps and offering excuse after excuse for why nothing ever materialized.

What is Your Motivation in Life?

TAKEAWAY Set goals for yourself and lay out how you plan to achieve them. Ultimately, it is up to you to take action and transform your goals into reality.

How Well are You Managing Your Brand?

Much of your success in life depends on how well you present yourself to others. Are you making poor decisions that are stifling your career development? If so, you may want to reevaluate how you are managing your brand.

Think of yourself as the CEO of your brand. Each time you step into an interview or clock in for another day at work you are promoting the most valuable commodity you have— yourself. Focus on three main points as you build your brand: 1.) use effective verbal communication, 2.) present an engaging image, and 3.) deliver when it comes to substance.

Use effective verbal communication– As CEO of your brand, the way you speak can open doors or slam them shut before you can get a foot in! Long before I ever had a plan for my future my mother told me to speak like I had a college degree. It took me a while to understand what she meant. My mother always stressed the importance of delivering my thoughts clearly and concisely. To her delight, I was

11

able to memorize speeches and deliver them everywhere from church to school and contests as well. I continued refining my speaking skills as new opportunities presented themselves. This groomed me for corporate meetings and also laid a solid foundation to be able to communicate effectively when teaching.

Present an engaging image– The second component is the image you project. This includes things like facial expressions, body art, hairstyle and the clothes you wear. Many times you are seen before you're heard. Following with this, then it is easy to see how others can form ideas about you based on your outer appearance.

Freedom of expression is a right which people take very seriously. Dress codes and traditional societal roles have become more relaxed to accommodate this increased focus on personal expression. No one can tell you how to dress or how to style your hair. Just remember, when someone is deciding whether or not to hire or promote you, you want to be evaluated based on what you bring to the table without your image interfering.

Deliver when it comes to substance– How many times have you heard that something looks good but lacks substance? Presentation can help you get a foot in the door, but substance is what separates the real from the fake.

The most successful companies go to great lengths to increase their edge over competitors. They find ways to execute business strategies more effectively than the competition. A company's ability to execute is indicative of the substance it is delivering to its stakeholders. From Coca Cola to Apple, top companies work tirelessly to add value to their brand. This may include exclusive partnerships, acquisitions, or developing new products. In the same way, you should strive to refine your core strengths. Today's competitive job market challenges you to harness every advantage at your disposal.

Ways you can add substance to your existing skills and abilities:

❖ Earn a college degree or trade certification that will help you pursue your interests,
❖ Shadow a mentor who has experience in your field of interest,

13

How Well are You Managing Your Brand?

❖ Pick up relevant work experience. Internships, work-study, and volunteer assignments can help you gain experience as you prepare for the next level, and

❖ Branch out. Expose yourself to other cultures and people from backgrounds different from your own.

TAKEAWAY Your brand is valuable.

Communicating your ideas clearly and effectively is an important part of your brand.

Also, be mindful of the image you present to others as it can either open doors to new opportunities or hold you back. Try to find that balance between being comfortable with your image and being presentable in professional settings.

Let substance be the backbone of your brand. Your ability to communicate and project yourself effectively to others is important, but style without substance is often futile. Make the most of opportunities to hone the skills you need.

6
Build Your Circle of Success

The mark of truly successful entrepreneurs and businesspeople lies in achieving sustained success. One-hit wonders are here today and gone tomorrow, but pioneers and moguls find ways to stay relevant. Having a strong network of driven individuals in place can provide a huge boost. Surrounding yourself with people who believe in you helps create an atmosphere that fosters success. This group is your circle of success. In case you haven't done it already, start assembling your circle of success immediately! An effective circle should reflect the three major parts of your personal journey– where you have been, where you currently are, and where you aspire to be. Balance is also important. Be careful not to stack your circle with too much influence from a particular part of your personal journey. For example, your circle of success would be less effective if it only reflected where you have been and did not include individuals who embody where you are and where you aspire to be.

Build Your Circle of Success

❖ **Where you have been** includes past experiences. Experiences from your past and lessons you have learned along the way influence how you approach life.

❖ **Where you currently are** includes those things going on in your life today. This may be school, work, existing goals, or projects you are working on.

❖ **Where you aspire to be** includes your aspirations and what you are working to achieve. For example, your 5-year career plan would clearly state what you plan to accomplish professionally within the next five years. It would also lay out progress checkpoints to help you stay on track.

Your circle of success should be more than a group of casual acquaintances. Seek out individuals who have skills, experience, and defining characteristics that you can build upon as you work to achieve your goals.

Suppose for a moment that you are looking to start your own business. You have sales experience and believe you can fill a niche distributing widgets online. Your circle of success consists of four members– Emily, Sophia, Matt, and Jack. Diagram 1 gives an example of a circle of success that would be in line with your entrepreneurial ambition. Notice how the members of your circle reflect the three parts of your personal journey. First up is Emily. Her position as a retail manager is in line with your past sales experience. Next, there is Matt. As a counselor, he can help as you prepare to start your business as well as down the road when you need advice on how to handle difficult situations. Matt's expertise puts him in two categories– 'where you currently are' and 'where you aspire to be'. Sophia's expertise as a web developer can help you design a website that suits your customers' needs. This lands Sophia in the where you aspire to be category as well. Lastly, as the owner of his own business, Jack represents where you aspire to be. His know-how as an entrepreneur makes him a good sounding board to bounce ideas off as you gather info and develop your own strategy. Together, Emily, Sophia, Matt, and Jack bring an ideal combination of knowledge, skills, and relevant experience to the table.

Build Your Circle of Success

TAKEAWAY Teamwork makes the dream work! When your circle of success is in place, stay in touch with each member. Group chats and conference calls can be great ways to brainstorm and generate ideas.

Assembling a network of motivated individuals whose attributes complement your goals will help you achieve sustained success.

30 Jewels

Diagram 1. Sample Circle of Success

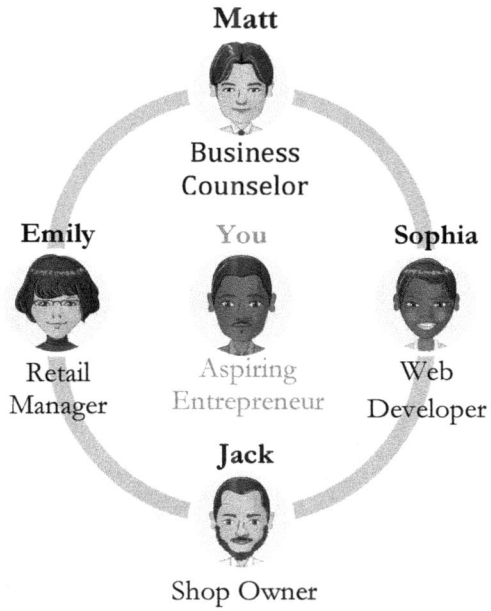

Matt

Business
Counselor

Emily   You   **Sophia**

Retail   Aspiring   Web
Manager   Entrepreneur   Developer

Jack

Shop Owner

Build Your Circle of Success

7 Tame Your Doubts and Fears

How much time do you spend worrying about things that are beyond your control? One of the easiest ways to miss out on great opportunities in life is to focus on all the ways you can fail.

Leaving Memphis to attend The University of Tennessee at Knoxville marked my first time being away from home and more or less on my own. I had to adjust to a big culture shock. By the time I turned eighteen I had witnessed drugs impact the lives of friends and family, lost people close to me to jail, experienced police profiling, and was familiar with gang violence. None of that prepared me for what would happen one day during my shift at a summer internship. I was interning at a Walgreen's just outside Knoxville. Assisting customers was a regular part of my responsibilities. One day as I approached a customer to ask if he needed help he looked squarely at me and asked me if my blood was the same color as my skin. Everything going on around me came to an abrupt halt. A million thoughts raced through my mind. I considered lifting him out of the wheelchair he was slouching in, but then I remembered I was at work and that would only jeopardize my internship. "OK then," I thought. "I'll take the high road and let the store manager know about the incident." When I told my manager he simply smirked and asked why it offended me. Being asked if my blood was the same color as my skin was sobering and my manager's reaction delivered a second dose of reality. Ultimately, the experience motivated me to push harder and reinforced my drive to succeed.

By this time I had completed my undergraduate degree and my sight was set on earning a Master's degree in Economics. I had already spent four years away from home in Knoxville and wanted to earn my Master's degree closer to Memphis. The University of Mississippi's strong Economics program stood out among other Mid-South institutions. I applied for admission and was offered a full scholarship including a housing stipend and additional pay to work as a graduate assistant. One thing about the opportunity concerned me, however, and that was Mississippi's reputation as a place where strained race relations are the norm. I did not know it early on, but the

Walgreen's incident would help me adjust to the social climate in Mississippi.

I remember watching a KKK rally take place just off campus. Even though the Klansmen were not wearing hoods and shrouds the demonstration embodied every bit of the hate-filled sentiment I had come to associate with the rallies from stories I heard growing up.

Then in 2008, Senator Barack Obama made history when he became the United States' first Black president. As it turned out, The University of Mississippi was the location of the first presidential debate of the 2008 election. I was on campus to experience the mixed feelings people had as President Obama laid out his platform. Emotions ran high and despite additional security detail, a doll with its face painted black was found hanging in a tree following the debate.

Despite how hard it hit me, the timing of that incident at Walgreen's could not have been better. It reminded me that there will be people who feel a certain way about me because of the color of my skin. Having gone through that and being able to make sense of it, I was prepared to make the most of my opportunity to attend The University of Mississippi.

While Memphis was what I knew from birth, stepping outside that comfort zone and taming my doubts and fears allowed me to excel in Knoxville and Mississippi and open doors to even bigger opportunities in Washington, D.C. In much the same way, you will be able to take advantage of opportunities in your own life when you conquer your doubts and fears.

TAKEAWAY   Go after each of your goals like you *know* you will succeed. Doing so allows you to focus on putting forth your best effort. If you are not doing this already, work this small change into your daily routine and you will be amazed by the difference it makes!

8 Crawl Before You Walk

Building momentum behind a new business or venture can seem impossible. I was faced with this dilemma while trying to jumpstart Prepared for the World youth mentoring. There I was with a head full of ideas about how Memphis communities could be improved and no formal training to suggest I knew how to accomplish such a serious undertaking. Few people and even fewer companies were in a hurry to support new organizations like mine. I knew that if the program was going to have any longevity I had to work even harder to learn the ins and outs. That work involved finding funding programs, gaining exposure, and managing the stacks of paperwork that come with operating a nonprofit.

Funding nonprofit programs can be costly. I made a pledge to myself that all the activities and programs would be 100% free for the families we helped. To keep that pledge I had to pay for many of the expenses myself during the early years.

Crawl Before You Walk

Exposure is important for any nonprofit. If donors don't know a program exists then how can they support it? That meant I had to get the word out about Prepared for the World. To address this I took advantage of every opportunity available to speak at schools, community centers, colleges, and churches to increase awareness. I also launched www.PreparedForTheWorld.org to spread the word online. As an added touch, I had t-shirts made to help make the program more visible.

Another thing I had to get used to was the huge amount of paperwork that must be filed to operate as a qualified nonprofit organization. Nonprofit organizations must report to federal agencies as well as state and local offices. I was hands on when it came to filing forms because I wanted to learn the business side of operating a nonprofit organization. Whenever I did not understand something I did my own research or asked someone who had experience preparing the required forms.

Persistence and hard work paid off and we eventually attracted both corporate sponsors and individuals who were glad to help the organization achieve its mission in the community. With that level of support Prepared for the World has been able to expand and benefit more children each year since its inception. *Desktop Repair and Komputer Education 101 (D.R.A.K.E. 101)* and *1,000 Books 1,000 Hours Literacy Program* are just two of the successful programs Prepared for the World now offers.

TAKEAWAY As you blaze new trails in life understand that everything may not fall in place immediately. Dig into your creative space to find ways to make up for what you lack.

Crawl Before You Walk

Go Hard Every Day

Treat each day like a new blessing; like another chance to improve and build regardless of what happened the day before. Try not to linger over missteps or past mistakes. When you see that you've gotten off track take note, regroup, and move forward. It is up to you to make the most of each day. Remember to acknowledge progress you make no matter how small it may seem.

Starting off, many of my accomplishments with Prepared for the World were small; like receiving a $100 donation from a corporate sponsor or filling twenty seats during our first panel discussion. I stayed with it because I knew that if I did there was a chance I could impact young children's lives. Giving back to the communities that helped raise me made it worthwhile. Year after year we expanded the programs offered and continually reached more youth. Prepared for the World is still active in the Memphis community. To this day, I am thrilled when former program participants tell me about the exciting things they are pursuing and the positive impact Prepared for the World had on their lives.

TAKEAWAY Do not write off the small accomplishments you make on the way to achieving your ultimate goal. Even a journey of a thousand miles begins with a single step.

10
Celebrate Other People's Blessings

All too often people are jealous of the good fortune in other's lives. As an ambitious individual, jealously has no rightful place in your life. It will make you bitter and prevent you from reaching your full potential.

If left unchecked, this gloom and doom frame of thought can easily turn into a crab-in-the-bucket mentality. For the proverbial crabs in the bucket it is especially hard to get ahead. Picture a bucket of crabs scurrying to make it to the top of the heap. Each has the same goal in mind– escaping to freedom– yet every time one comes close to escaping it is pulled back in. It's almost as if the crabs are saying to each other, "If I can't get ahead then neither can you." Be careful not to adopt this toxic way of thinking. Before you get salty about the next person's good fortune consider applauding his or her accomplishments.

When you believe and trust that there is a purpose for your life then you will find that there are unique blessings assigned to you and you alone. This opens the door for you to appreciate other people's good

Celebrate Other People's Blessings

news like it is your own. The real beauty of taking a genuine interest in someone else's good news is in the positive energy you generate. When you share positive energy with others they tend to do the same. This system of exchanging heartfelt support will build you and those around you up.

TAKEAWAY Be happy for other people's blessings. Don't allow jealousy to corrupt your personality and tarnish relationships. Be happy for other people's highpoints in life. Learn from the crab-in-the-bucket analogy and build people up instead of tearing them down.

30 Jewels

11

Help Others Reach New Heights

It is easy to approach life with a closed fist mindset, holding on tightly to the things you already have, especially when you're focused on coming up. A closed fist may not lose anything, but more importantly a closed fist cannot *receive* anything.

I recognize how blessed I am and believe it is my responsibility to be a blessing to others. This led me to create Prepared for the World youth mentoring to help at-risk youth. Its mission is to provide at-risk youth the resources and guidance needed to become leaders in their communities. My involvement with the children, their parents, and volunteers has enriched my life more than I can describe. When you approach life in this manner you will be amazed by how many hands and hearts open up to you.

You have probably heard the saying 'It's lonely at the top'. That is not entirely true. 'The top' is only lonely when you turn your back to others on the way up. While everyone who is on your team today may not be with you in the long run, there is plenty of room for old friends and new connections.

How often are you helping those around you reach new heights in their lives? When you are dealing with genuine people and you show interest in where they are going they tend to reciprocate and take interest in you. The stronger your team is the better off you are.

TAKEAWAY Adopt and apply the open hand approach to life. Take pride in helping others. Helping others goes beyond money. Knowledge and understanding are very valuable. Being in a position to share what you know and impact the lives of others is priceless.

12

Find a Healthy Outlet

From time to time stress may mount. Stress is your body's way of responding to 'high alert' situations. In this sense, it is a defense mechanism. When your body queues this high alert signal under normal conditions you are able to tackle difficult tasks like taking an exam. During a tough exam your level of concentration might be heightened to help you recall what you studied the night before. Sports are another area where stress kicks in to help you perform under pressure. In the final seconds of a ball game, stress may trigger your body to produce the adrenaline you need to sink the winning shot.

While stress is a natural response to certain situations, prolonged periods of stress can have severe repercussions including emotional distress, fatigue, ulcers, and weight gain.

Handling stress effectively can yield huge benefits. There are many healthy options to choose from. You may, for example, find that reading takes your mind off work-related stress. If you lead a more active lifestyle you may prefer a brisk jog. Choose an outlet you enjoy that fits your lifestyle and keep stress in check. In addition to reducing stress, outlets like reading and jogging have other benefits. Reading regularly can improve cognitive skills. [†]Physical activities can help you lose weight and regulate blood pressure and cholesterol.

TAKEAWAY Confront stress head on by doing more of the healthy activities that can help you release tension. Ignoring signs that your stress level is unusually high could be stacking the odds against you. Consult your physician before making changes to your regimen.

13
Never Mind the Haters

Some people will doubt, criticize, speculate, and project negative energy your way. Sometimes everyone won't be in your corner. This hit home even more during my campaign for District 87 State Representative in my hometown Memphis, TN. I was 26 and excited to be stepping to the plate to run for office. I was fully vested in my bid to bring job growth to a slice of my city that needed positive change.

Despite all this, a few people close to me told me I may as well drop out of the election because I would not win. I asked myself, "How is it that they see me working day after day to improve my community and still do not support the movement?" What I learned is that everyone will not see your vision, especially if you are pursuing goals that are different from their goals and what they believe is possible in their own lives.

In the end I did not win the election, but the campaign opened so many doors for me that it is hard to view it as anything but a success. The experience allowed me to connect with a lot of good people which means a lot to me because I love my city.

TAKEAWAY Don't limit yourself to what other people think is best for you. Outside support is great, but be prepared when it falls short of what you need. This is when you must dig deep and push forward. After all, who knows how badly you want to succeed better than you?

14
You Only Fail When You Stop Trying

As you grow in life learn to embrace challenges that pop up. Try not to think of obstacles you experience along the way as stop signs. Instead, think of them as instructions on how to improve and learn from them. All too often we let these challenges and our own mistakes discourage us from reaching the finish line. Don't be discouraged. Pump your brakes and reflect on the situation. Are you doing something that may be stifling your progress? Maybe there is a better approach you could be taking. Stepping back and assessing your progress may reveal that you are close to a breakthrough.

Mistakes are part of the game, so do not dwell on mistakes you make along the way. As long as you learn from them and try not to repeat them then each attempt brings you closer to your goal.

TAKEAWAY Never give up. When you recognize that challenges and mistakes are part of the process you will learn to adjust while keeping your goals in focus.

You Only Fail When You Stop Trying

Set goals for yourself. You may find it helpful to start by setting small goals that you can accomplish in a short period of time and work your way up to bigger goals that take longer to accomplish. Be just as dedicated while pursuing the long term goals as you are when chasing your short term goals.

15
Dare to Dream

'Shoot for the stars. If you miss you'll land in the clouds.' You have probably heard this saying many times. The message is simple– aim high! Your dreams represent what you are passionate about and where you aspire to be in life. Embrace your dreams. Ask yourself what it is that you really want in life.

A link exists between dreaming and achieving. That link is belief. Belief compels you to take action even in the face of uncertainty. When you believe you will cross the finish line you are willing to grind through whatever obstacles lay in your way. Envision yourself being so committed to achieving your goals that all you think of is realizing them. By channeling your thoughts and psyche you can set yourself on a path to achieve your wildest dreams.

Great things can happen when you focus your efforts and apply yourself. At the same time, it is often difficult to focus when you have too much going on. Before you take aim at the stars streamline your efforts. You can do this by creating a list of goals and ranking them from the most urgent to the least important. Next, list the activities that mean the most to you (i.e., spending time with family, hanging out with friends, etc.). Your top three goals and the three most important activities make up your focus list. The idea is to sync your goals with the activities you engage in. You may find that your dreams have not become reality because you are splitting your time between too many activities. Your focus list may also reveal that the activities you currently dedicate the most time to go against some of the goals you have set. Take inventory of how you spend your time and adjust your schedule to reflect the goals and activities that rank high on your focus list.

TAKEAWAY Dare to dream and refuse to settle. Create a focus list to rank your goals and prioritize your activities. You may find that you need to make changes to your routine. Time is something you cannot get back. Eliminate activities that crowd your schedule.

Part 2

Kenneth Woods

16
Make It Happen

When I was seven years old my parents got divorced. Seeing my family fall apart hit me pretty hard. One second everything seemed fine and the next we were having family meetings where my mom and dad explained what was happening. I remember crying and saying, "I won't do it anymore," as if they were getting divorced because of something I did.

After the split was final my mother, my younger brother, and I moved in with my aunt while my mom worked to get us in a house of our own. This was a tough time for all of us. Everyone had to make adjustments. Almost overnight my brother and I went from getting picked up after school to taking care of ourselves in the evening. Seeing my mother work so hard to make ends meet made me want to help. Her effort to provide for us helped me understand that along with money came security. From that point on I began looking for ways I could earn money. Like many kids my age, my first hustle was selling candy. I put together my own operation selling candy at school and it was putting cash in my pockets. Wow, what a rush! Things were going well until one day when the principal confiscated my candy. Unfortunately, selling candy was not allowed. Just like that I was out of the candy business.

Nevertheless, I had tasted success and was hungry for more. Even more important than the money I earned from selling candy was a valuable lesson I learned– a successful entrepreneur identifies what his or her customers want but do not have access to and finds a way to deliver.

While there was little I could do to bring my parents back together, seeing that I could organize my own operation and earn money solidified in my mind that my current situation did not determine how far I could go in life.

TAKEAWAY Some of life's changes can be difficult to accept. Do not underestimate your ability to rise to the occasion when you find yourself in uncharted waters. Brilliant ideas and untapped potential are inside you waiting to be unleashed.

17
Read Life's Road Signs

Some people believe we are products of our own environments. Others believe in destiny and say a successful person would be successful no matter what cards life dealt. Before I ever considered whether we are products of our surroundings or whether destiny determines our paths I recognized that I could learn a lot from the people I came in contact with every day. I applied this to individuals who were making positive strides and also to those who were not on the up and up.

Very quickly, I observed that the successful people I knew had some things in common. The common denominator was education. Most of the individuals I knew who owned businesses and led successful careers had earned college degrees or completed specialized training or trade certification. This let me know that I needed to take my education seriously.

There was no shortage of examples of what not to do in my neighborhood. The good thing about this is that I could learn from their mistakes and avoid the bumps and bruises they took along the way. For example, I saw drug addicts walk the same blocks day after day and saw their bodies and minds waste away. This showed me that drugs only lead down a dead end road. I also saw a lot of my peers getting pregnant. Many times both the female and her partner would drop out of high school in order to provide for the baby. I knew I was not ready or able to provide for a child. Seeing this scenario play out time after time helped me get my priorities in focus.

TAKEAWAY Don't think you have to learn everything the hard way (i.e., through trial and error). You can pull life lessons from the individuals around you and apply them to your own life. When you apply lessons learned from other people's experiences you free up more time to focus on getting ahead as opposed to playing catch up.

18
Follow Your Passion

When you are putting your game plan together it may seem like everyone has suggestions about what you should do. Do not fret, though. Some of that advice may be good. There's nothing like being able to go to someone you trust and receive sound advice. Suggestions aside, though, amazing things are possible when you tap into your own passion.

I am a strong believer that everyone has a purpose in life. Your real journey begins when you identify your calling. Following your passion can take you in places you never imagined you would go.

When I was studying at The University of Tennessee there came a time when I had to choose between the degree I was working toward and my career passion. Originally, my major was Finance with Internal Auditing collateral. These are both solid degree tracks. My dilemma was that I chose them based on how much money I stood to make after graduating. The more I reflected on my interests the more I realized my heart was not into Finance or

Follow Your Passion

Auditing. I knew I did not want to make a career doing that kind of work.

After much debate, I changed my major to Enterprise Management with collateral in Marketing during my junior year. Even though the change pushed my graduation date back my new degree path complemented the things I was passionate about. The knowledge and skills I acquired set me up to land a great career position with BNSF. Making the difficult decision to change my major and follow my passion paved the way for me to land a career I enjoy.

TAKEAWAY Your true passion is tied to the purpose-driven life you are meant to live and is worth pursuing.

19
Stay Down 'til You Come Up

It is very rare that the payoff comes overnight. You may even find yourself feeling like you have endured one journey only to be taken through another. That is how I felt when I looked to enter the job market in 2007.

I remember it like it was yesterday. I was a year from graduating and I was beginning to think about the new responsibilities I'd have once I graduated. That list of new responsibilities included finding a place to live, paying student loans, and landing a job. I felt like there was a huge clock counting down over my head.

After the spring term ended I returned to Memphis and jumped in head first, looking to land anything that paid. I applied to dozens of positions. While I did land some interviews, I was not getting any offers and time was passing. This made me doubt whether I would find a good job. Nevertheless, staying prayerful gave me the resolve to stick with the process.

Stay Down 'til You Come Up

Submitting applications online was not panning out, so I decided to adjust my approach. I threw on my suit, printed some copies of my résumé, and hit the pavement. I was motivated and ready to prove how I would be a great hire to each company I contacted. Success! I received three interviews on the spot and two job offers that day. "At last," I thought. It seemed I was making some headway.

This relief did not last long, though. Once again, my excitement was met with a dose of reality– none of the jobs paid much. On top of this, rejection letters for other positions I applied for were beginning to roll in. Somehow I could feel that something was about to give. I kept telling myself, "I can do all things through Christ who strengthens me." Later that month I was extended a management internship with a major retailer that would pay $500 a week. The internship was slated to begin at the end of the summer.

Things got even better. Not even a full week after being offered the retail internship, I received a call from Burlington Northern Santa Fe Rail (BNSF) offering me an internship in Minneapolis, MN. The

BNSF internship was in line with my Enterprise Management degree so I jumped at the opportunity. The pay was nearly double what I stood to earn with the retail internship plus I received a housing stipend. I still enjoy working for BNSF so I would say my situation worked out for the best!

TAKEAWAY   Do not give up on the process. Hold your head. If your approach is not delivering the results you want you may find it necessary to make changes.

Stay Down 'til You Come Up

20
Expect More

Expectations reflect what you believe will happen at some point in the future. People from just about every walk of life set expectations. Parents, wanting the best for their children, look forward to seeing them excel in school and extracurricular activities and going on to be productive members of society. Managers are concerned with productivity so they expect employees to hit performance standards. Students set their sights on graduating and form expectations regarding class performance to help power themselves toward the finish line.

The same applies to you personally. Expectations you set for yourself can influence what you achieve (or fail to achieve). If you don't set expectations for yourself, or if the expectations you set are too low then your results will likely be less than stellar. This is because expectations set the standard for how vigorously you pursue your objectives. Will you set the bar low and not rise to your full potential or will you expect more from yourself and discover what you are really capable of achieving?

53

Expect More

TAKEAWAY   As you explore your true potential, look for areas where you can raise the bar.

21
Maximize Your Moment

There are 60 seconds in a minute and 60 minutes in an hour. That means there are 86,400 seconds in each day. Regardless how you use your time, each second has one thing in common with the other 86,399 seconds in the day– once it ticks off the clock you cannot get it back. Time is precious so make the most yours.

TAKEAWAY Maximizing your 'moment' involves taking advantage of opportunities and making good use of the resources that are available to you. It is up to you to be ready when your time to shine comes. Second chances are not promised so take your best shot the first time.

Maximize Your Moment

22
Complacency is Your Worst Enemy

Think of complacency as getting too comfortable; falling back when it is really time to go in. You may recognize it by one of its other names– 'I'm good', 'Maybe next time', or 'Eh, I just don't know'. Regardless which name you recognize, they all have the same effect which is allowing you to find security in inaction.

The thing about complacency is that it creeps up on you when you least expect it. This takes me back to one of my proudest moments which was buying my first home for my 24th birthday. I was the youngest homeowner in a nice neighborhood. Thinking back on how I had to move in with relatives as a kid brought a huge smile to my face. That period of early struggles had such a profound impact on me that I felt I had come full circle.

I have no doubt that purchasing a home was a great achievement. It also marked a major shift in how I saw things. My drive and motivation faded. I felt I could relax for a while and enjoy the benefits of my hard work, so relax I did. More and more of my time was spent partying and going out. I allowed myself to get too comfortable and had convinced myself I was 'good' having made it to where I was.

Don't get me wrong. All the parties and trips were fun, but overdoing it set me back. I eventually decided I wanted to get into real estate investing. I remember feeling like an athlete who had not played in a while. My initial efforts were clumsy and lacked coordination. Similar to how an athlete has to get back in playing condition after a hiatus, I had to get back in the habit of grinding!

TAKEAWAY   Live life and enjoy the benefits of your hard work. Just don't allow yourself to get complacent. Keep your mind active and stay engaged.

23
Expand Your Hustle

In 2009 the Great Recession sent shockwaves around the world. Companies laid off employees in record numbers. Some companies even turned to the government for assistance as economic conditions worsened. Millions of households were unable keep their homes and resorted to foreclosure. From that devastation a sort of 'new normal' emerged.

While households and companies are still adjusting, the US economy appears to be showing signs of life again. However, employees are not finding the same jobs that existed before the recession. Instead, firms seem to be relying more on part time employees and temporary staff to satisfy their demand for labor. As a result, many employees are seeing their benefits disappear.

In light of these changes, resourceful workers are searching for ways to recover income lost during the Great Recession and in some cases earn more. Some are taking on second jobs. Others are exploring their creative abilities and developing products that fill pockets of consumer demand (e.g., mobile apps).

Expand Your Hustle

TAKEAWAY Welcome to the 'new normal' where job security is largely a thing of the past. Expand your hustle by creating alternate sources of income and increase your financial independence.

24
Losses are Part of the Game

Short term losses play an important role in realizing long term gains. Think of them as day-to-day progress reports. When the reports show that you are not doing so well then you know it is time to make some changes. Making adjustments here and there keeps you on track to hit your goals.

I've suffered my share of losses. None stand out more than the string of losses I took when I invested in a nightclub in Springfield, MO. The club promoter was a friend of mine. He came to me seeking a loan so he could make some necessary repairs and restock inventories. The agreement was that after six months I would receive a 100% return on my investment for my role as a silent investor, so I figured this was a win-win. That is where I was wrong.

I took the bait and loaned my friend the money. Shortly after that I found myself coming out of pocket to cover miscellaneous expenses as well. "No biggie," I thought, "I am still in for a huge return on my initial investment." Again I was wrong. Business got slow and he leaned on me to drive traffic to the

Losses are Part of the Game

struggling night spot. I slowly realized I had made a mistake in investing my time and money into such a poorly run venture. This was his first time operating a club. I felt like I was hanging on while the business crashed and burned.

My efforts to turn the club around did have some impact. Locals and college students started showing up. However, one problem still remained– the promoter was not motivated to pick up where I left off and run the club. This was my wakeup call that I needed to cut my losses.

TAKEAWAY Making mistakes and taking some losses is unavoidable. However, repeating the same mistakes only compounds your losses.

25
Be Investable

Some people recognize the importance of sharing what they know and embrace mentorship. The key to attracting quality mentors is presenting yourself as being investable. People want to know that their time and efforts are having a positive impact, otherwise what is the point? In the beginning a mentor looks for potential. Then as that mentor works with her apprentice she expects to see progress.

When I first considered getting involved with real estate I wanted to learn from the best Springfield, MO had to offer. I was usually able to find the contact info of real estate professionals in plain sight on advertisements. Sure enough, one of the investors I called was willing to take me on as an apprentice. I was shocked when I learned that his real estate holdings represented 3% of a local bank's entire real estate portfolio. He helped me learn the ins and outs of real estate by allowing me to shadow him. I also looked for other opportunities to pick his brain. This level of exposure to a major investor who was active in the Springfield market shortened my learning curve a lot.

As time passed I became better at identifying deals. My mentor recognized this and included me in even more business. He even purchased my first property. My share of the profit from the deal was $5,000. I did two other deals in Springfield before relocating to Fort Worth, TX. Other investors I met while in Springfield have expressed interest in doing business with me in the Dallas-Fort Worth, TX market off the strength of what I accomplished with the help of my mentor. I progressed from a novice into a property wholesaler who was good at connecting motivated sellers with investors who were willing and able to purchase their homes.

TAKEAWAY Good mentors possess invaluable experience you can apply to reach your goals. Being investable is about how well you go from showing potential to showing progress.

26 Explore the World

Traveling exposes you to new cultures, and amazing experiences. It allows you to see how other people live. Once you have taken all these things in you can compare them to what you are accustomed to. You may return home more focused and motivated to go even harder.

There are many ways to gain overseas exposure. A relaxing vacation may be your ticket abroad. If you don't want to drop a lot of scratch traveling there are other options available to help you explore the world. Many universities encourage students to participate in volunteer excursions into foreign lands. Also, Au Pair and similar programs place individuals in foreign households for short periods of time. Depending on your line of work, your employer may make overseas assignments available.

Whether your trip is for business, leisure, or volunteer purposes it is likely you will see and experience things that will leave a lasting impression on you.

Explore the World

TAKEAWAY Take advantage of opportunities to travel abroad and experience different cultures. The new connections you make can enrich your personal growth and development.

27
Make Your Money Work for You

Growing up I was taught the importance of saving. My parents would tell me, "Don't spend all your money. Save some for a rainy day." Their instructions stayed with me over the years and to this day I make sure I set a portion of what I earn aside for emergencies, ordinary expenses, and retirement. After paying bills and making sure I have enough money to carry me in case of emergency I invest what is left.

It may be your goal to enjoy a retirement full of traveling or maybe you would like to spend your days restoring classic automobiles. Regardless what you look forward to doing start plotting your course to achieving that ideal retirement today. Make sure you are not so focused on the here and now that you are neglecting your future financial security.

Income can be divided into three categories—active income, portfolio income, and passive income.

Active income is income you work to earn. Salaries, wages, tips, and commissions are included in active income. As its name suggests, active income requires you to be directly involved. There are only 24 hours in a day, so you face a tradeoff between how much active income you earn and how much leisure time you enjoy.

Portfolio income includes interest, dividends, and capital gains. These payments can come from stocks, bonds, or time deposit accounts. Each is relatively easy to purchase.

Passive income is derived from business partnerships or ventures you have a stake in but do not share in the routine operations or physical upkeep. This type of income is not limited by how many hours you work. However, it may require a larger upfront investment (e.g., a significant cash down payment is required to purchase an investment property).

Throughout the rest of this jewel the focus will be on portfolio income. Think of portfolio income as a bridge between active income and passive income. Remember, for active income there is a tradeoff between income and leisure time. The same tradeoff between income and leisure time does not exist for passive income, but the large upfront commitment may present an obstacle.

When it comes to creating a portfolio income stream there is no shortage of options. Before you deploy any funds there are four basic points to consider– setting your investment goals, doing the research, assessing risks, and taxes.

Investment Goals

Are you interested in establishing a steady stream of income or would you like your money to grow faster? Your goals will help shape the strategy and portfolio allocation that is most ideal for you.

Stocks and bonds are two common investment classes. Mutual funds are another investment class. On the savings front, there are many kinds of time deposit accounts to choose from including money market accounts (MMAs) and certificates of deposit (CDs).

Shares of stock represent portions of ownership in a company. When companies want to raise funds they can make blocks of shares available for purchase.

Make Your Money Work for You

Some companies choose to pay investors dividends. Dividends are regular payments (usually every three months) that are made to shareholders by companies. Dividend-paying stocks can bolster your portfolio income.

Bonds represent debt. Companies as well as all levels of government use debt financing to generate funds to pay for capital expenditures and ongoing operating expenses. Bonds pay interest to the holder for a designated length of time (known as the term). At the end of the term the principal amount is typically repaid to the bond holder, although it is possible for the term to be extended. Sometimes companies issue convertible bonds that can be converted into shares of stock.

Mutual funds allow investors to invest in baskets of stocks, bonds, and time deposit products. This spreads the risk associated with any given fund. Mutual funds pay dividends and capital gains distributions as well.

Time deposit accounts are bank accounts that require accountholders to deposit funds for a fixed term. These savings products are insured against bank default.

Doing the Research

There are many reputable financial websites you can use to do research and build an investment strategy that fits your goals. Most have interactive tools that let you track certain holdings and create sample portfolios to test your skills before you put real money behind your picks.

Assessing Risk

Determining your risk tolerance is very important. Risk is associated with expected return on investment. The higher the risk an investment the higher the expected return. Your risk tolerance describes how sensitive you are to losing money. If you find you have a low tolerance then you may consider safer investments like investment grade bonds, FDIC-insured time deposit accounts, or blue chip stocks. If your risk tolerance is higher you may be open to owning shares of a new and unproven company.

Micro-lending is another option if you have a bigger appetite for risk. Micro-lenders lend relatively small amounts of money to borrowers who are not able to borrow funds through traditional lending channels like banks. Micro-lenders receive higher interest payments to compensate for the riskier nature of the loans they make.

Keep in mind that the prices of stocks fluctuate based on company specific data and market data. These fluctuations can negatively impact the value of your investments.

Bonds represent debt. When bondholders purchase bonds they run the risk that the borrower defaults and can no longer make interest payments or worse yet cannot repay the principal amount that was borrowed.

Tax Treatment

Portfolio income is subject to taxes just like active income and passive income. Different investments may have different tax treatment.

Consult a financial advisor and your tax professional to learn more about specific investment strategies that fit your needs.

TAKEAWAY [1]A well-managed portfolio income stream can help you achieve the level of financial security you desire. Portfolio income can complement your active income and also serve as a great building block towards creating passive income. Plus, it is money you do not have to punch a clock to earn!

Diagram 2. Risk Scale

US Gov't Bonds   *Mutual Funds*   *Stocks*

Less Risk   *More Risk*

Make Your Money Work for You

28
Even if it is Free it will Cost You

People tend to want to get the best deal possible. There's a certain feeling that comes along with knowing you 'stuck it to the man'. Getting a good deal depends on how good you are at assigning value. Value can be a tricky thing to measure. Value describes how much a product or service is worth. Whether you know it or not, you assign value to any number of things on a daily basis.

Price is probably one of the first things you consider when deciding whether to buy an item. The price you pay for an item can impact how you feel about the purchase itself. For example, if you were shopping for a leather jacket you would probably feel good if you paid $99 for a jacket you believed was worth $200. On the other hand, if you paid $299 for the same jacket you might walk away with buyer's remorse.

Understanding how to assess fair value for the products and services you use can save time and money. While overpaying is never ideal, being too price-conscious can cost you as well. That is because cheaper doesn't necessarily mean better. Say, for example, you came across a knock-off that only cost $49 and looked identical to the leather jacket mentioned above. As you decide which jacket to purchase you need to consider the pros and cons of each. Table 1 lists the main points you would need to consider.

Assume the leather jacket's actual price is $99. If you bought the knock-off then you would save $50. However, as Table 1 shows, your decision should be based on more than price alone. The quality of the material is another factor to be considered. You would expect the knock-off to be made of less durable materials which means it probably would not last as long as the leather jacket. Keeping with this reasoning, let's say the leather jacket has a product lifespan of three years while the knock-off has a product lifespan of six months. This changes things quite considerably. When you factor in how long each jacket will last the $49 knock-off becomes the [2]more expensive choice.

Whether you end up with a stylish leather jacket or a knock-off is not important. What really matters is your value system. Understanding that you get what you pay for and being able to form accurate expectations about the products and services you buy are necessary for wealth creation.

Just because something is cheap does not mean it is a good deal. On the other hand, a higher price does not necessarily indicate higher quality.

Even in the absence of prices you assign value. How is this possible? It's simple; your time has value. Whenever you allocate time to one activity over another you are saying that the activity you chose has a higher time value than the activity you forwent. So the next time you kick back and watch TV you are placing a higher value on watching TV than whatever else you could be doing.

TAKEAWAY It can take time to learn how to spot quality and assign fair value. You get what you pay for. Maintenance costs and replacement costs may not show up on the price tag, but they do add to the effective cost of ownership.

Even if it is Free it will Cost You

At minimum, even a 'free' offer will cost you some amount of time (more than likely it will require you to spend some money as well).

Table 1

	3-year Cost	Pros	Cons
Leather Jacket	$99	More durable, Lasts longer	Higher up-front costs
Knock-off	$249	Looks similar to leather jacket, Less expensive (up front)	Less durable, May not last as long

Even if it is Free it will Cost You

29
Be a Game Changer

Game changers are individuals who revolutionize the way others view their area of expertise. You may have some entertainment icons, musicians, or business executives who you consider game changers in mind.

The same applies to companies and the products they sell. In many industries there is an 'it product' that consumers like and prefer over competing products. These products may lead the pack today, but they must continue impressing consumers or they will be old news tomorrow. This process of improving upon existing products and introducing entirely new products is called innovation. Innovation is continually reshaping the world as we know it.

Game changers are finding creative ways to thrive in today's global marketplace. The emergence of social media platforms like Twitter and Facebook has made the exchange of ideas virtually uninhibited. This phenomenon has led to the creation of exciting new companies and products as well as emerging industries.

81

Be a Game Changer

In this highly competitive environment, firms that are not able to compete will be surpassed by industry leaders or go out of business completely. Similarly, individuals who are not equipped to compete may find it difficult to advance in their professions.

TAKEAWAY   Industries are evolving at a breakneck pace. Technology and globalization are connecting people and markets like never before. Tap into your creativity in order to take your craft or career to the next level.

Run the Score Up

Being successful in life comes down to one thing–
perfecting your process. As the saying goes, there's
more than one way to skin a cat. It's all about how
you are going about achieving whatever goal you have
set for yourself. An example of a process is someone
working part time to pay for college. Once that
student graduates she may land a full-time career
position. This would reflect a change in her process.

Regardless what the process is its function
remains the same. A process is simply a means to
your desired end. Prioritize your goals and develop a
process that works for you. As long as it delivers
results stick with it. The second it stops delivering or
when you recognize you can be working smarter, look
to make some adjustments to your process.

This can be applied to nearly anything, but for
simplicity let's use money. Say you want to stack
$10,000. If this seems overwhelming then it may help
to look at your goal a little differently. In this case,
you can measure how effective your process is in
terms of how many pay periods it takes to reach your

goal. This small change in your approach can play a big role in your ability to save $10,000.

Consider the following scenarios in Table 2.

Table 2

	Gross Pay	Taxes/Expenses	Savings
[3]Scenario 1	$800	$700	$100
[4]Scenario 2	$1,538.[46]	$1,346.[15]	$192.[31]

In Scenario 1 you earn $10/hr. Applying that to a 40 hour work week means you would earn $400/wk. and $800 per pay period. Of course taxes will be deducted and you will also have expenses to cover. In the end, you have $100 free and clear to put toward your $10,000 goal.

Saving $100 each pay period in Scenario 1 means it would take 100 pay periods to reach your goal of $10,000. That's nearly four years!

$100 per pay prd. x 100 pay prds. = $10,000

By now, you may be interested in seeing how earning more (changing your process) can help you save $10,000 in less time. Scenario 2 shows you just that. In Scenario 2 your earnings increase from $10/hr. to $40,000 a year. The same expense assumptions from Scenario 1 have been applied to Scenario 2. For example, tax still represents 20% of gross income. After accounting for taxes and expenses you would be left with $192.[31] in Scenario 2.

Saving $192.[31] each pay period in Scenario 2 means it would take 52 pay periods. By refining your process you have reduced the time it takes to save $10,000 down to 2 years. That is a huge difference from the time it took in Scenario 1.

$192.[31] per pay prd. x 52 pay prds. = $10,000.[12]

With your goal to stack $10,000 behind you, you may decide you want to save another $10,000. This time, though, you are interested in putting it together in even less time than it took in Scenario 2. By now you know that if your goal changes then you need to change your process as well. You have two options:

❖ Earn more (e.g., getting a raise or picking up a second job) and

❖ Spend less (e.g., reducing miscellaneous expenses or taking on a roommate to lower rent).

It may take time to increase your earnings, so let's see how reducing your expenses can help you accomplish your new goal of stacking $10,000 in less than two years. Let's assume there is nothing you can do to reduce your taxes and you can only reduce how much you spend on rent, food, and other expenses. In Scenario 2 expenses (excluding taxes) represent $1,038.[46] (67.5%) of your budget. That is a huge chunk of your income! Making some small changes to your expenses can help you stack the next $10,000 quicker. In Scenario 2 we assumed the following expense breakout: housing– 30%, food– 25%, and other expenses– 12.5%.

Now consider the following adjustments:

❖ Take on a roommate to cut housing expenses in half,

❖ Reduce food expenses by 5%, and

❖ Reduce other expenses by 7.5%.

Let's call this Scenario 3. Table 3 shows your expense breakout after making these adjustments. As it illustrates, your savings after taxes and expenses would equal $615.^{38}. Saving this amount each pay period in Scenario 3 means it would take just over 16 pay periods to accrue $10,000. By refining your process and cutting some expenses you have reduced the time it takes to less than one year.

$$ \$615.^{38} \ per \ pay \ prd. \ x \ 16.25 \ pay \ prds. = \$10,000.^{58} $$

Table 3

	Gross Pay	Taxes/Expenses	Savings
Scenario 2	$1,538.^{46}	$1,346.^{15}	$192.^{31}
[5]Scenario 3	$1,538.^{46}	$923.^{08}	$615.^{38}

TAKEAWAY A process is simply a means to one or more ends. The key to 'running the score up' in life is understanding how and when to adjust your process. As your goals (i.e. your ends) change then the process (i.e. the means) you apply must also change.

30 Jewels

The Core Themes of 30 Jewels

Successfully navigating life's twists and turns is no small task. Plus, everyone's circumstances are unique. The jewels presented throughout this book are based on the following core themes which we believe form the foundation of every purpose-driven existence. If you would like to see how a core theme relates to a particular jewel then go to the page numbers provided.

Belief— Great things are possible when you believe.

❖ Increase your chances of success by surrounding yourself with people who believe in you (pp. 15–19).

❖ Hold firm and believe there is a special purpose for your life. There are unique blessings assigned to you and you alone (pp. 29–30).

❖ Embrace your dreams and believe in your ability to make them your reality (pp. 39–40).

❖ Difficult times can force you to dig deep (pp. 43–44).

The Core Themes of 30 Jewels

❖ Be confident in your ability to rise to new levels (pp. 53–54).

Perseverance– Stay the course. Do not be discouraged by setbacks.

❖ Nothing worth having comes easy. Unexpected hurdles may pop up as you progress toward your goals (pp. 29–30).

❖ You only fail when you stop trying (pp. 39–40).

❖ Do not let hard times break your spirit. Instead, use them to power you to success (pp. 43–44).

❖ Put your objectives in front of you and go to work. Cloudy skies eventually give way to sunshine. Similarly, difficult periods in life often pass (pp. 49–51).

❖ Nothing worth accomplishing comes easy. Learn from your losses and apply what you learn going forward (pp. 61–62).

30 Jewels

Patience– Curb your anxiety. Your breakthrough may take time to develop.

❖ Be prepared in case your plans are slow to take off. Understand that they may take some time to unfold. Stick with the process (pp. 3–4, 5–7).

❖ Sometimes short term sacrifices are necessary to achieve your long run goals (p. 9–10).

❖ Save time and frustration by learning from the mistakes of others. (pp. 45–46).

❖ It may take time to discover what your passion in life is, but the time is worth it because your passion is linked with the purpose-driven life you are meant to live (pp. 47–48).

❖ Transitioning into the workplace can be difficult. Researching the companies you are interested in and building a neat, concise résumé can increase your chances of landing a great position. (pp. 49–51).

The Core Themes of 30 Jewels

Goodwill– Step up to the plate and help others.

❖ Helping others does not deprive you of what is meant for you (pp. 31–32).

❖ Building others up can benefit you (pp. 33–34).

❖ Keep your pride in check. Be open to advice others offer based on their life experiences (pp. 45–46).

❖ Good mentors are willing to share their wealth of knowledge and experience with others. Your advice and guidance may be exactly what the next person needs to get ahead (pp. 63–64).

❖ Embrace other cultures (pp. 65–66).

Time management– Your time is valuable. Once it is gone you can't get a second of it back. Make the most of each day.

❖ Do more than talk the talk. Develop a plan and spring into action (p. 9–10).

❖ Engage in activities that will sharpen your skills and knowledge base (pp. 11–14).

30 Jewels

❖ Do not waste time worrying about things you have no control over (pp. 21–24).

❖ Set time aside for things that can enrich your life (pp. 35–36).

❖ Make the most of the resources available (p. 55).

❖ Don't slack off when you get a taste of success (pp. 57–58).

❖ Tap into your creativity and revolutionize the game (p. 81–82).

Positive energy– Think positive. Be positive. Let the world see you at your best.

❖ Focus on finding the solution instead of allowing yourself to become overwhelmed by the problem (p. 2).

❖ Learn to share in other people's happiness (pp. 31–32).

❖ Find healthy ways to decompress and prevent stress from pushing you to your limit (pp. 35–36).

The Core Themes of 30 Jewels

❖ Be open to constructive guidance, but do not entertain negativity (pp. 37–38).

Empowerment– You can achieve anything you dedicate yourself to.

❖ Explore new ways to apply your skills and boost earnings (pp. 59–60).

❖ An experienced mentor can help you develop both personally and professionally. (pp. 63–64).

❖ Putting your funds to work with investments that suit your risk tolerance can give you more control over your time and deliver the financial security you need (pp. 67–74).

❖ Price isn't the only thing you should consider when making purchases. Learning how to spot value is an important part of wealth creation (pp. 75–80).

❖ Develop a process that allows you to make steady progress. (pp. 83–88).

Appendixes

Make Your Money Work for You

Appendix 1

[1]The information provided is for educational purposes only and is not a recommendation to purchase, sell, or consider the securities mentioned. Do your own research to learn the risks associated with specific investments. Past performance is no guarantee of future results. Investments may lose value. Consult a financial advisor and a tax professional to determine your specific investment needs.

Even if it is Free it will Cost You

Appendix 2

[2] $294 total cost of knock-off is based on a 6-month lifespan across a 3-year period.

$49 each * 3 years * 2 knock-offs per year = $294

Appendixes

Run the Score Up

Appendixes 3–5

[3,4]Expenditure calculation assumes taxes are 20%, housing is 30%, food is 25%, and other expenses are 12.5% of gross income. Does not account for accrued interest. Also assumes a 26 pay period work year.

[5]Expenditure calculation assumes taxes are 20%, housing is 15%, food is 20%, and other expenses are 5% of gross income. Does not account for accrued interest. Assumes there are 26 pay periods in work year.

About the Authors

About the Authors

Justin Settles was born and raised in Memphis, TN. He earned a BA in Economics from The University of Tennessee at Knoxville and a MA in Economics from The University of Mississippi. In 2006 Justin founded Prepared for the World youth mentoring program. Prepared for the World is a qualified 501(c)(3) nonprofit organization. The organization continues to mentor and lift up at-risk youth throughout Memphis and Mid-South.

Justin is passionate about Memphis and in 2010 he ran for the position of Tennessee District 87 State Representative at the age of 26.

He currently works as an economist for the US Bureau of Economic Analysis in Washington, D.C. As a federal economist, Justin conducts research that improves the quality and completeness of BEA publications.

Justin is also an Economics instructor at the GraduateSchoolUSA. He enjoys teaching and sharing his passion for Economics with students. When asked what he likes most about teaching, Justin replied, "I appreciate the opportunity to exchange ideas with people from backgrounds different than my own."

He remains committed to helping youth overcome obstacles and become positive figures in their communities and serves as Executive Director of Prepared for the World.

About the Authors

Kenneth Woods is a product of Memphis, TN. He graduated from The University of Tennessee at Knoxville.

Kenneth is currently Manager of Customer Support at Burlington Northern Santa Fe Railway for the Dallas, TX market. He has been with the company since 2007.

He also created K Woods Investments, LLC in 2012 and continues to manage its operations today. Kenneth has found success brokering wholesale real estate deals.

Kenneth is an active member of Phi Beta Sigma, Inc. He strives to lead by example and encourages others to make the most of what they are blessed with.